Fire Modeling Institute
Missoula Fire Sciences Lab, Missoula Montana

USDA

2013 Annual Report
Fire Modeling Institute

Fire, Fuel, and Smoke Science Program
Missoula Fire Sciences Laboratory
Rocky Mountain Research Station
U.S. Forest Service

Application

Information

Modeling

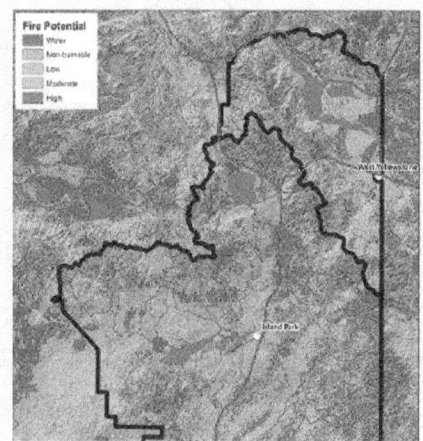

Edited by Robin J. Innes, Faith Ann Heinsch, and Kristine M. Lee

Table of Contents

Introduction

Highlights by Branch
Application Team

Information Team

Modeling Team

Introduction

Fire Modeling Institute

The Fire Modeling Institute (FMI) of the U.S. Forest Service, Rocky Mountain Research Station (RMRS), is a national and international resource for fire managers. Located within the Fire, Fuel, and Smoke Science Program at the Missoula Fire Sciences Laboratory (Fire Lab) in Montana, FMI helps managers utilize fire and fuel science and technology developed throughout the research community to address land management problems.

The staff at FMI works with a range of national and international partners, including other agencies, state and local governments, academia, and nonprofit groups. The information and technology developed by FMI is available to the public for its benefit and use. This issue of FMI's Annual Report summarizes the results of activities for 2013. Information about FMI projects, data products, and applications can be accessed at http://www.firelab.org/fmi. FMI is funded largely by Washington Office Fire and Aviation Management.

The three branches of FMI—Application Team, Information Team, and Modeling Team— provide different roles and assistance to managers and scientists in the application of fire science.

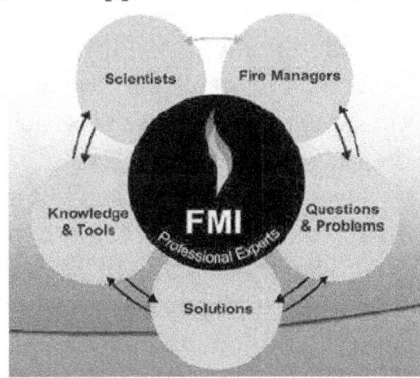

Application Team

The Application Team provides analysis, development, training, and support in fire behavior, fire ecology, modeling, and fuel treatment effectiveness. It is comprised of technical experts from the Fire Lab and the national LANDFIRE program. The Team works directly with managers on current fire-related land management problems.

Information Team

The Information Team is comprised of ecologists and technical information specialists at the Fire Lab. The team develops scientific literature reviews and other synthesis documents on fire effects and historical fire regimes. All products are published in the Fire Effects Information System (http://www.fs.fed.us/database/feis/). To support synthesis preparation, the Team also maintains a comprehensive library of fire ecology research and an online library catalog, the Citation Retrieval System (http://www.feis-crs.org/).

Modeling Team

The Modeling Team is comprised of specialists in fire behavior, fire ecology, and forestry at the Fire Lab. The Team maintains and develops a suite of fire behavior modeling systems that includes BehavePlus, FireFamilyPlus, FARSITE: Fire Area Simulator, and FlamMap. They manage the operation, support, and expansion of the Wildland Fire Assessment System (WFAS) and the Weather Information Management System (WIMS). They also develop and support systems used in analyses by the Application Team.

Figure: FMI's mission is to connect fire managers, technical experts, and scientists with the best fire analysis technology and with the most current information from the scientific literature available to respond to their fire-related resource management needs. FMI provides a variety of services to clients including project design, data analysis, literature review and synthesis, software training, spatial analysis, workshops, and technical advising.

Analyzing the Past to Prepare for the Future: Methods and Lessons Learned in Fire Behavior Modeling in Bulgaria

A team from the Rocky Mountain Research Station and the Bulgarian Academy of Sciences began a collaborative project in 2013 to identify and describe various fuel types for the Zlatograd Municipality in southern Bulgaria, as well as to establish methods for modeling recent wildfires. Several datasets that classify vegetation in Bulgaria were available, including paper maps displaying vegetation in 1991, high-resolution orthophotos from 2011, and paper and spatial vegetation maps from the local municipal forestry department. However, Bulgaria lacks classified fuels data necessary to perform fire behavior simulations using any available fire behavior model.

FMI Fire Behavior Analyst LaWen Hollingsworth, Fire Spatial Analyst Greg Dillon, and Physical Scientist Faith Ann Heinsch sought to adapt an available fuels classification (by identifying appropriate fuel models) to the Zlatograd Municipality for use in two fire behavior modeling systems developed in the United States (FARSITE: Fire Area Simulator and BehavePlus) to analyze the spread of past wildfires. Neither of these things had ever been done for Zlatograd or any other Bulgarian municipality.

Information for 15 wildfires that occurred during 2011-2012 within the Zlatograd Municipality was included in the fire behavior modeling effort. The wildfires were fairly small but caused the deaths of four volunteer firefighters. Methods for analyzing fire behavior and fire growth using fire modeling systems from the United States were established,

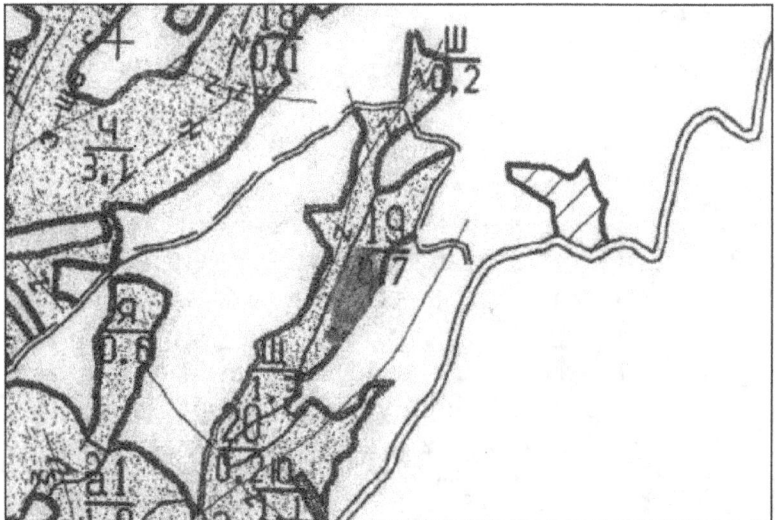

Top figure: Paper map of a fire in Scotch pine forest provided by the Zlatograd Forestry Department. Bottom figure: Paper maps were digitized and the starting point (yellow circle) and final shape (solid red polygon) of the forest fire along with vegetation type polygons showing prefire vegetation (red lines) were overlaid onto background orthophotos. Figures courtesy of Nina Dobrinkova, Bulgarian Academy of Sciences.

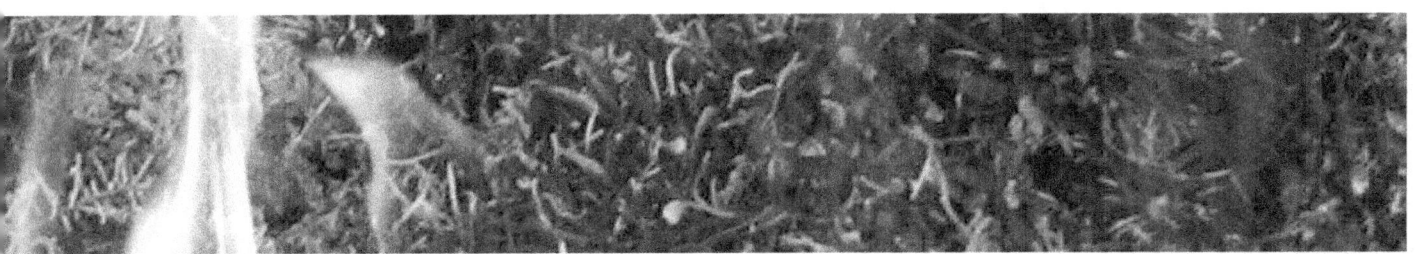

and through this process, shortcomings in the systems were identified, most notably with how they deal with metric data.

Applying standard fuel models within fire behavior systems developed elsewhere can be difficult. FMI researchers were able to identify several fuel models from the United States that seemed compatible with Bulgarian surface fuels. However, when these fuel models were applied to the Zlatograd Municipality, the model results were inaccurate. Simulations would require fewer assumptions if data specific to each fire, including prefire vegetation, suppression actions, fire weather observations, and observed fire behavior (such as flame length, rate of spread, direction of growth) were available. Inaccurate weather data was a major cause of inaccuracy. Weather data in Bulgaria must be purchased and is expensive.

Having easier, more affordable access to weather station data would substantially improve future fire behavior simulations, even if no additional information were available. The availability of such data would allow comparison of modeled fire behavior with observed fire behavior and improve the accuracy of simulations.

Contact: LaWen Hollingsworth
FMI Staff: Greg Dillon, Faith Ann Heinsch, LaWen Hollingsworth
Collaborator: Nina Dobrinkova (Bulgarian Academy of Sciences)
Status: Ongoing

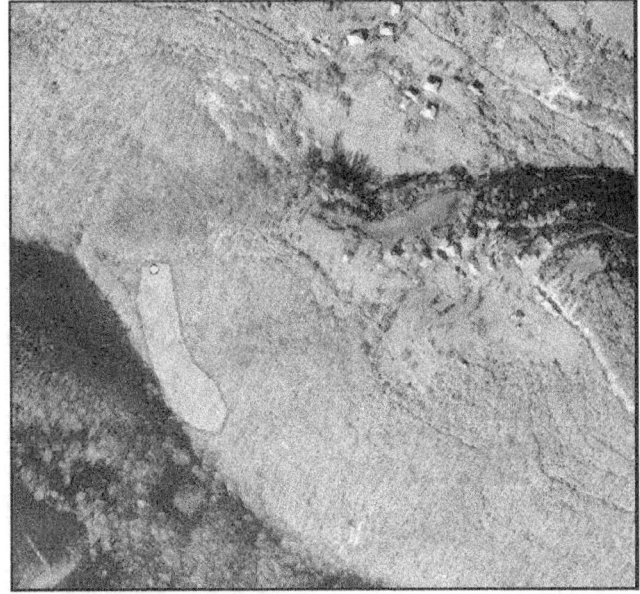 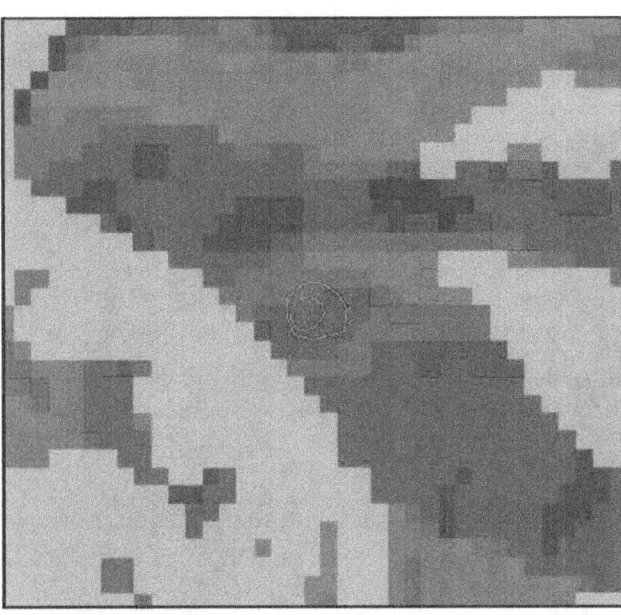

Left figure: The starting point (yellow circle) and final shape (red polygon) of a wildfire that burned in a European beech forest in the Zlatograd Municipality. Figure courtesy of Nina Dobrinkova, Bulgarian Academy of Sciences. Right figure: A FARSITE: Fire Area Simulator run for the forest fire. Blue concentric lines indicate the projected fire size.

FEAT-FIREMON Integrated

FEAT-FIREMON Integrated (FFI) is an interagency, science-based, ecological monitoring software application that is designed to assist managers in meeting inventory and monitoring requirements as mandated by Federal law and agency policy. It is used in the U.S. Forest Service, National Park Service, Bureau of Land Management, U.S. Fish and Wildlife Service, U.S. Geological Survey, Bureau of Indian Affairs, and by Tribes, state, and local governments, nongovernmental organizations, and universities.

FFI uses plot-based data collected using a variety of sampling protocols to consistently describe ecological systems and monitor change over time. It incorporates the components necessary to conduct a successful monitoring program, including an integral database, analysis and reporting tools, and modular GIS component.

The FFI development team is nearing completion of FFI-lite, a SQL Server CE-based version of FFI. This new application was developed in response to user requests for a version of FFI that is easier to install and manage. While FFI-lite does not allow multiple simultaneous users like FFI does, it includes the full complement of error checking, data form customization, and reporting tools found in the full version of FFI, and will be the desired application for units with smaller monitoring programs that do not need the functionality of a SQL Server-based application. An additional benefit is that FFI-lite can be used for collecting electronic data on field computers, eliminating the time needed to copy data from hardcopy field forms into FFI and reducing the opportunity for data entry errors. Additionally, a new GIS toolbar compatible with Arc GIS 10.1 was distributed in 2013.

Members of the FFI development team presented a four-hour workshop at the Fifth International Fire Ecology and Management Conference in Portland, OR, and a four-day training course at the Southern Area Advanced Fire and Aviation Academy in Birmingham, AL. The four-day course included two field days covering field sampling and data collection methods and two classroom days providing hands-on instruction with FFI software.

FFI technical support is accomplished through the FFI Google discussion group, email, and phone "help desk". The FFI technical support lead in FMI recorded more than 120 technical support contacts in 2013.

Contact: Duncan Lutes
Collaborators: National Park Service, Systems for Environmental Management, Axiom IT Solutions
Status: Ongoing

Figure: Field studies in ecological monitoring with FEAT-FIREMON Integrated. Photo courtesy of Duncan Lutes, FMI.

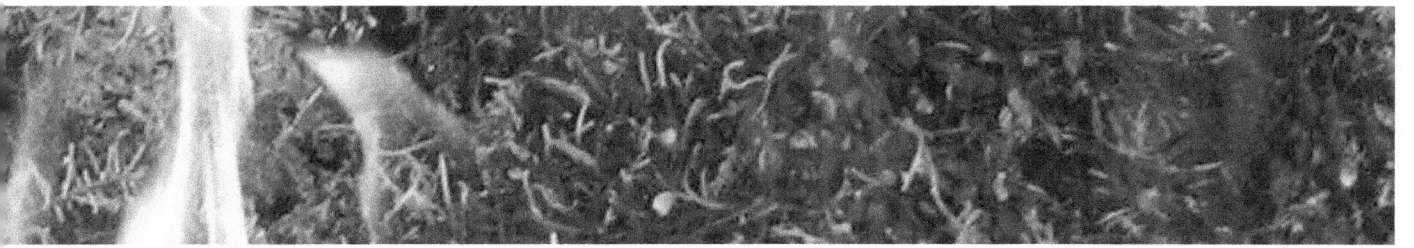

Hazardous Fuels Prioritization and Allocation System

The Hazardous Fuels Prioritization and Allocation System assists the U.S. Forest Service, Washington Office, Fire and Aviation Management (WO FAM) staff by helping guide the distribution of hazardous fuels funding among U.S. Forest Service Regions. Members of the Fire Modeling Institute, WO FAM and the U.S. Forest Service, Pacific Northwest Research Station collaborate each fiscal year to complete the analysis at national and regional scales.

The decision process takes into consideration the following factors: wildland fire potential, population density, smoke emissions, water supply, and performance measures. These data elements are compiled at a national spatial extent for input into Criterium DecisionPlus (CDP), a decision model. CDP assigns priority scores to each region based on the importance assigned to the data elements by an expert panel. Data and models are available to regional level managers who wish to use them to help guide fuels funding allocation within their regions.

This year, the HFPAS analysis process was improved in several ways. First, classes of the new Wildland Fire Potential Map were incorporated to characterize high and very high wildland fire potential. Second, decision model elements within a zone of intersection were assessed for areas with high or very high wildland fire potential in a manner consistent with risk assessment methodology. Lastly, new administrative boundary spatial layers created by the U.S. Forest Service Automated Lands Project were incorporated. These improvements will help to improve regional-level prioritization strategies.

Contacts: Jim Menakis, Frank Fay (WO FAM)
FMI Staff: Eva Karau
Collaborators: WO FAM, Pacific Northwest Research Station
Status: Analysis results, models, and data are delivered each fiscal year.

Figure: FMI Ecologist Duncan Lutes leads a classroom training session during the FEAT-FIREMON Integrated training course at the Southern Area Advanced Fire and Aviation Academy in Birmingham, AL . Photo courtesy of Duncan Lutes, FMI.

Quantifying Wildfire Risk to Structures in the Island Park Sustainable Fire Community

The communities of Island Park, ID, and West Yellowstone, MT, are situated just outside the western entrance to Yellowstone National Park amid grasslands, sagebrush, and aspen and conifer forests. As part of the broader interagency

Fire Potential
- Water
- Non-burnable
- Low
- Moderate
- High

Cohesive Wildfire Management Strategy policy created in response to the FLAME Act of 2009, a collaborative group called the Island Park Sustainable Fire Community (IPSFC) formed to develop a dynamic long-term strategy for a 314,000-ha (750,000-acre) area encompassing the two communities. The IPSFC recognized the need to evaluate the existing wildfire risk in the area to facilitate prioritization efforts for future fuels treatment projects designed to modify fire behavior.

FMI Fire Behavior Specialist LaWen Hollingsworth and RMRS Fire, Fuel, and Smoke Science Program (FFS) Research Ecologist Russ Parsons, in collaboration with U.S. Forest Service Region 1/Region 4 and Caribou-Targhee National Forest, assisted the IPSFC in developing a risk assessment. Risk of wildfire was evaluated and classified based on three components: likelihood, intensity, and effects. Likelihood of wildfire was classified using burn probabilities from the Large Fire Simulator (FSim), a system used to estimate burn probability and variability in fire behavior across large landscapes. Fire intensity is summarized using flame lengths from the geospatial fire behavior system, FlamMap. Burn probabilities and flame length data were combined to produce a map of wildfire potential across the landscape.

The effect, or value, is supplied by structure hazard assessments within the project area conducted in the Island Park and West Yellowstone communities. These data detailed ingress, egress, building materials,

Figure: Landscape fire potential for the Island Park Sustainable Fire Community project area.

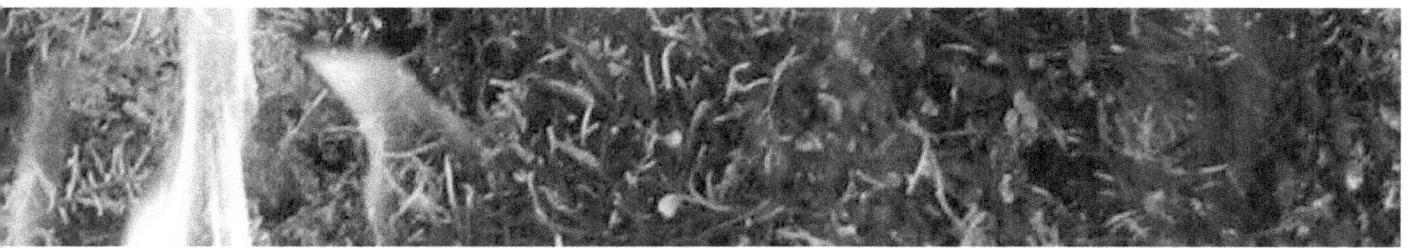

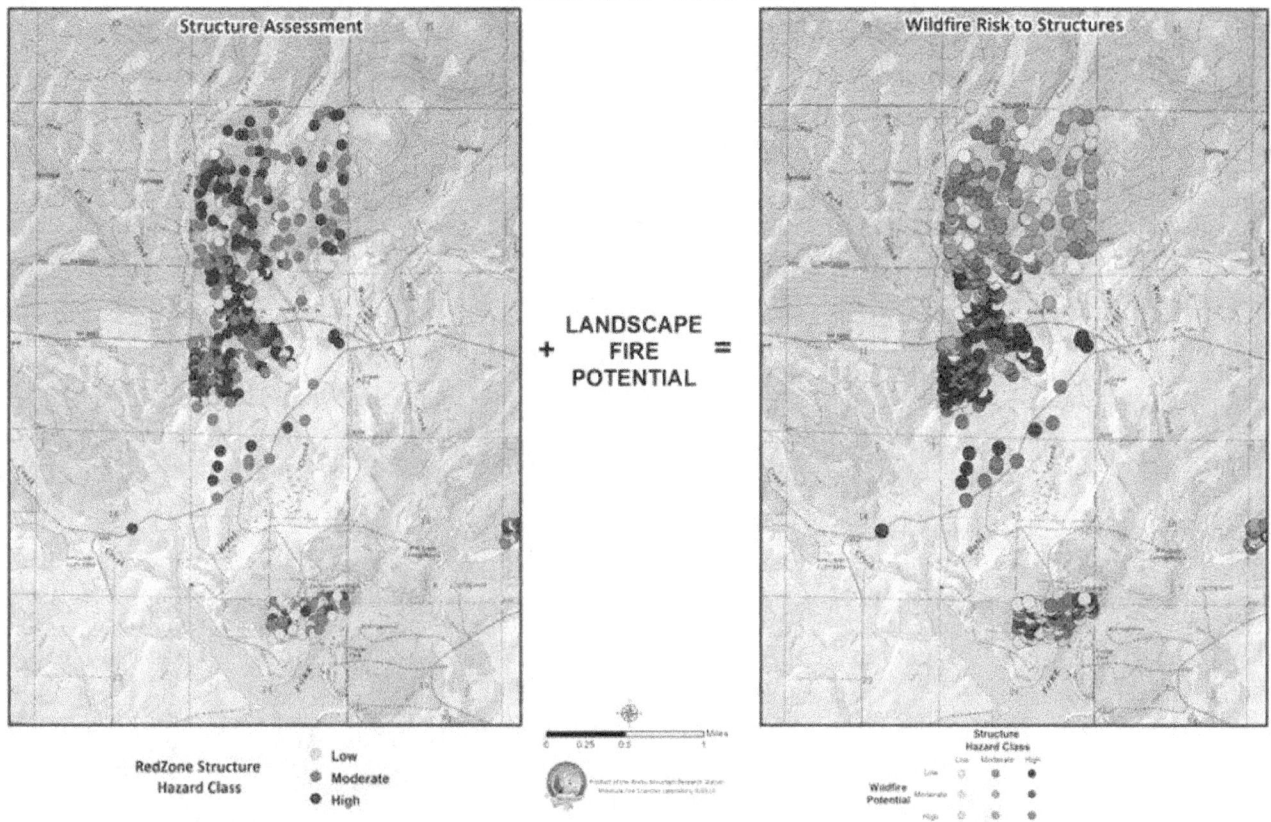

Island Park Sustainable Fire Community
Wildfire Risk Assessment - Yale Creek Area

and hazards adjacent to structures such as overhanging vegetation or propane tanks. The structure assessment data were classified into low, moderate, or high structure hazard classes, which were then combined with the landscape wildfire potential data to create a matrix displaying the wildfire risk to structures. The risk assessment data will be used by IPSFC to evaluate and prioritize fuels projects and inform homeowners of potential risks from wildfires and their responsibilities to mitigate those risks.

Contact: LaWen Hollingsworth
Collaborators: Liz Davy (Caribou-Targhee National Forest), Craig Glazier (Region 1/Region 4), Russ Parsons (RMRS Fire, Fuel, and Smoke Science Program)
Status: Phase I complete. Technical support ongoing.

Figure: The wildfire risk assessment map for the Yale Creek area, part of the Island Park Sustainable Fire Community project area located directly north of Island Park Reservoir.

Severe Fire Potential Map

Throughout 2013, FMI analysts continued work on the Severe Fire Potential Map, part of the Fire Severity Mapping Tools (FIRESEV) project. Work focused primarily on technology transfer activities.

In winter, the FIRESEV website at FRAMES (www.frames.gov/firesev) was launched to serve geospatial data for the Severe Fire Potential Map and supporting documentation. The final report for the FIRESEV project was submitted to the Joint Fire Sciences Program and made publicly available at http://www.firescience.gov/projects/09-1-07-4/project/09-1-07-4_final_report.pdf.

In spring, FMI analysts and RMRS scientists presented a seminar at the Missoula Fire Sciences Laboratory on the FIRESEV project and the Severe Fire Potential Map. A recording of the seminar is available at http://videos.firelab.org/ffs/2012-13Seminar/030713Seminar/030713Seminar.html.

In summer, FMI analysts contributed to a feature story on the FIRESEV project for the Rocky Mountain Research Station's *Science You Can Use Bulletin* (http://www.fs.fed.us/rm/science-application-integration/docs/science-you-can-use/2013-07.pdf) and presented on the Severe Fire Potential Map and the FIRESEV project during a *Science You Can Use* webinar. In addition, FMI Spatial Fire Analyst Greg Dillon submitted a poster titled "Potential for High Severity Fire: a New 30 m Raster Dataset for the Western United States" at the Environmental Systems Research Institute International User Conference.

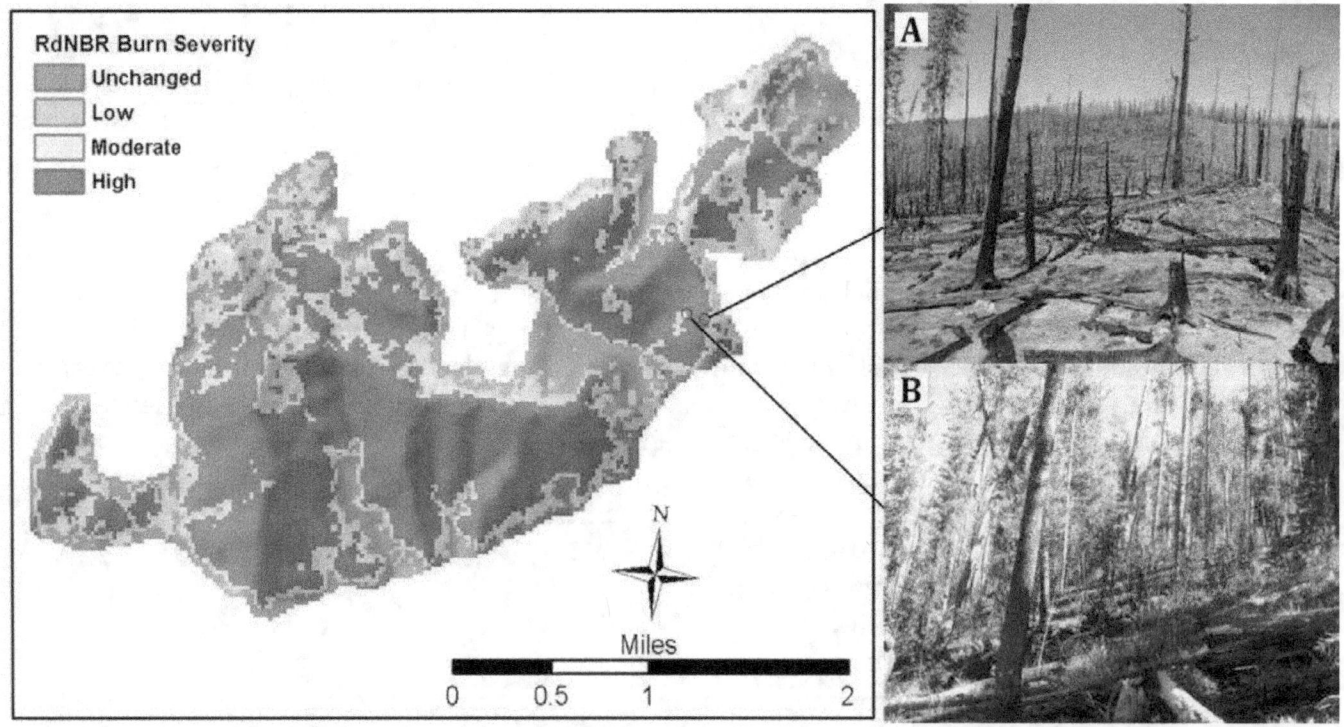

Figure A map of burn severity for a single fire obtained from satellite imagery. This kind of data was used to create the Severe Fire Potential Map. Photo A illustrates high-severity fire effects with overstory mortality and consumption of most surface fuel. Photo B illustrates low- to moderate-severity fire effects, with needle scorch on some trees and only partial consumption of surface fuels.

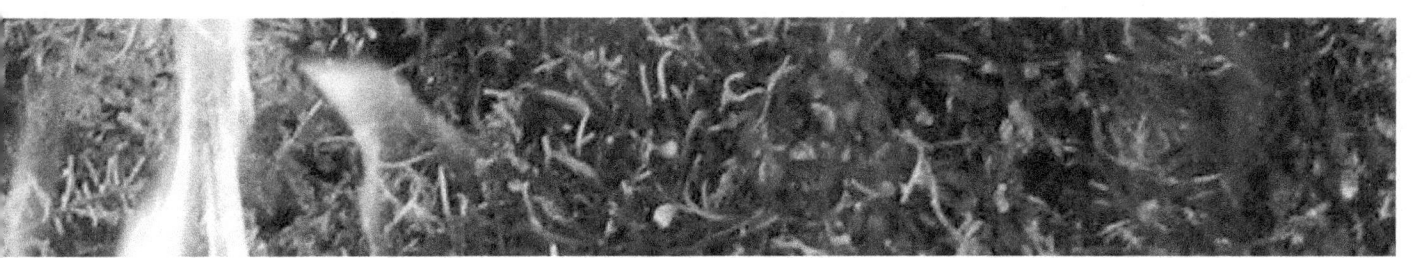

A Publication of the US Forest Service Rocky Mountain Research Station | July/August 2013 · ISSUE 6

Seeing Red: New Tools for Mapping and Understanding Fire Severity

In fall, the composite burn index field data and photos collected for the Severe Fire Potential Map were officially published on the U.S. Forest Service Research Data Archive (http://www.fs.usda.gov/rds/archive/Product/RDS-2013-0017).

Contacts: Greg Dillon (FMI), Bob Keane (RMRS Fire, Fuel, and Smoke Science Program)
FMI Staff: Greg Dillon
Collaborators: RMRS Fire, Fuel, and Smoke Science Program, University of Idaho
Status: Ongoing documentation and technology transfer

Figure: FMI analysts contributed to a feature story on the FIRESEV project for the Rocky Mountain Research Station's "Science You Can Use Bulletin".

Wildland Fire Potential Map

The Wildland Fire Potential (WFP) map is a raster geospatial product covering the conterminous United States that can be useful in assessments of wildfire risk or hazardous fuels prioritization at broad geographic scales. The WFP map builds upon, and integrates, estimates of the probabilistic components of wildfire risk developed via simulation modeling for all Fire Planning Units across the United States by RMRS scientists.

In 2013, FMI Spatial Fire Analyst Greg Dillon developed an updated version of the WFP map, and released it on a website where users can download GIS data, map graphics, and supporting documentation (http://www.firelab.org/fmi/data-products/229-wildland-fire-potential-wfp).

Since its release, the updated WFP map has garnered significant local and national attention, leading to direct technology transfer contacts with users from a wide array of entities, including the U.S. Forest Service, Bureau of Land Management, Bureau of Indian Affairs, Department of Interior, National Fire Protection Association, Xcel Energy, and USAA Insurance.

The Environmental Systems Research Institute (ESRI) created a GIS map service for WFP and featured it in their online Wildfire Public Information Map. Greg Dillon presented an award-winning poster on the WFP mapping process at the 2013 ESRI International User Conference.

As a product built on simulation modeling outputs from RMRS scientists, the WFP map provides a perfect opportunity for FMI to highlight the foundational work being done by U.S. Forest Service research in the arena of wildfire risk assessment. In the coming year, FMI will continue to provide technology transfer and application of the latest risk assessment science through the WFP map and other risk assessment products.

Contacts: Frank Fay, Jim Menakis (Washington Office Fire and Aviation Management)
FMI Staff: Greg Dillon
Collaborators: RMRS Human Dimensions Program, RMRS Fire, Fuel, and Smoke Science Program, Washington Office Fire and Aviation Management
Status: Ongoing
Presentation: Dillon, G. 2013. Wildland fire potential 2012: a tool for wildfire risk assessment and hazardous fuels prioritization. Poster presentation at the ESRI International User Conference, 8-12 July 2013, San Diego, CA.

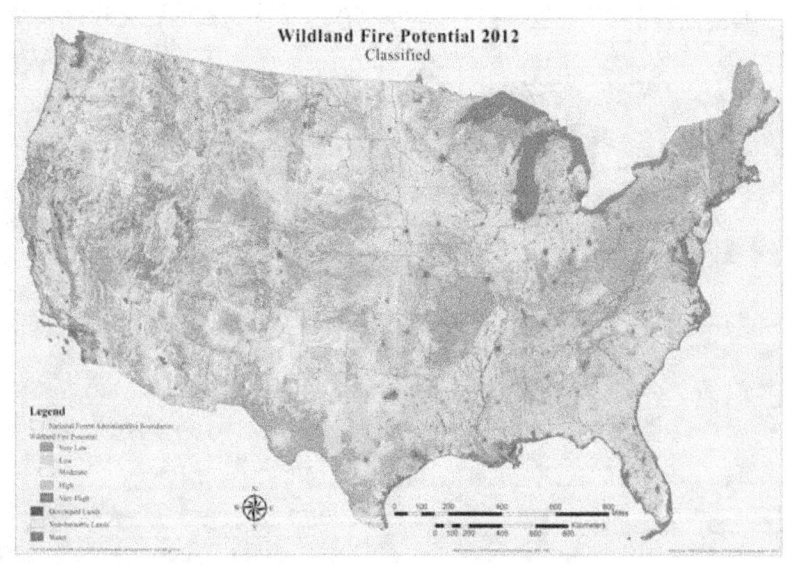

Figure Wildland Fire Potential (WFP) map classified into very low, low, moderate, high, and very high WFP classes .

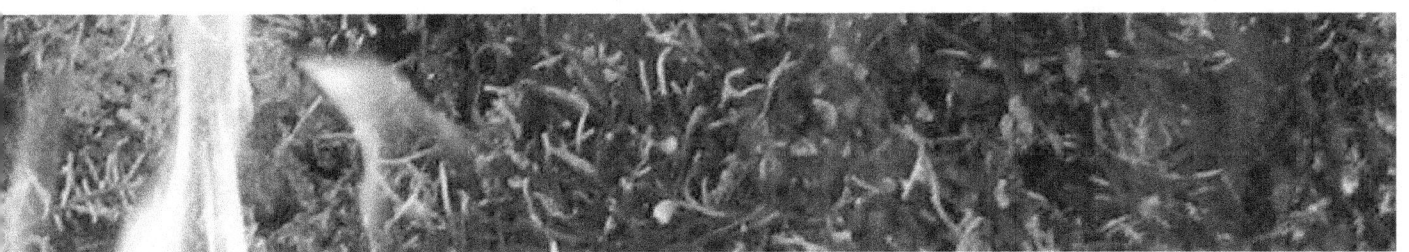

LANDFIRE 2010 Product Updates

LANDFIRE, also known as Landscape Fire and Resource Management Planning Tools, is a joint program between the wildland fire management programs of the U.S. Forest Service and the U.S. Department of the Interior. LANDFIRE applies consistent methodologies and processes to create comprehensive spatial data and models describing vegetation as well as wildland fire and fuel characteristics across the entire United States. LANDFIRE data products facilitate national, regional, and large landscape-level fire planning activities and provide managers with data needed for fire planning and implementation using a collaborative, cross-boundary, interagency approach.

In 2013, FMI-LANDFIRE staff continued to develop the production and delivery plan for the LANDFIRE 2010 data products. This included coordinated processing and delivery of refined and updated LANDFIRE 2010 vegetation products for the continental United States including existing vegetation, vegetation transition, and potential vegetation. FMI-LANDFIRE staff also coordinated and implemented LANDFIRE 2010 innovations oriented toward future versions of data, including fuel loadings classification and mapping; landscape change classification and mapping; and increased collaboration with Gap Analysis Program, National Vegetation Classification System, and Rocky Mountain Research Station specialists. FMI-LANDFIRE staff continued development of LANDFIRE methods and process documentation for modifying the LANDFIRE website

(http://www.landfire.gov/) and continued summary and documentation of LANDFIRE processes and products. Information on the LANDFIRE 2010 data products was presented at the Fifth International Fire Congress in Portland, OR, and the Fourth Fire Behavior and Fuels Conference in Raleigh, NC.

FMI-LANDFIRE staff participated in development of a production and delivery plan for the LANDFIRE 2012 effort. Items discussed included creation of a Vegetation-Transition Team, After Action Review

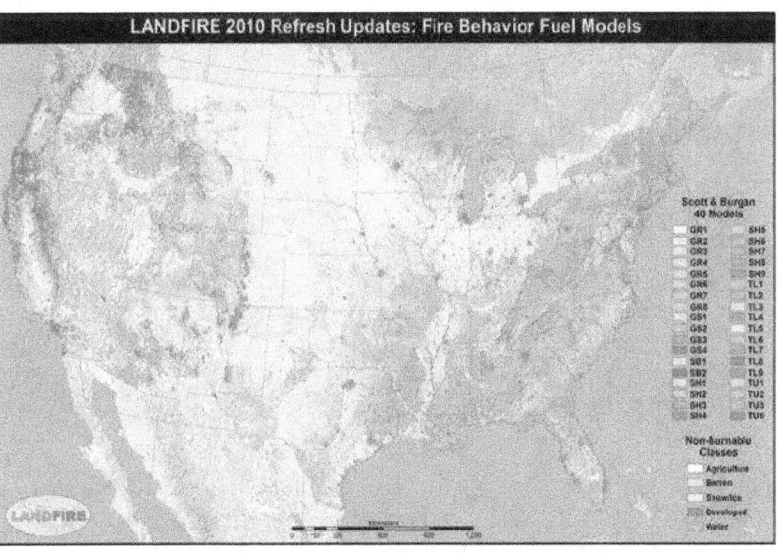

for the LANDFIRE 2010 effort, methods for revising and attributing the product suite, and production scheduling and staffing.

Agency Contact: Frank Fay (Washington Office Fire and Aviation Management)
FMI Staff: Don Long
Collaborators: Washington Office Fire and Aviation Management, U.S. Department of the Interior
Status: Ongoing

Figure: The LANDFIRE 2010 version of the 40 Scott and Burgan Fire Behavior Fuel Models for the conterminous United States.

Information Team

New and Updated Species Reviews and Fire Studies in the Fire Effects Information System

The Fire Effects Information System (FEIS, http://www.feis-crs.org/beta/) continued to serve managers in 2013, its twenty-eighth year. FEIS provides online syntheses of scientific knowledge about more than 1,100 species and their relationships with fire. Reviews cover plants and animals throughout the United States, providing a wealth of information for resource management, restoration, rehabilitation, and fire management.

FEIS had 557,524 visitors in 2013, an increase of 22% over the previous year. The system had visitors from all of the United States, with most visits from Washington, Oregon, California, Texas, Florida, and New York. FEIS received visits from more than 120 countries outside the United States.

Fourteen reviews covering 16 species were published in FEIS in 2013. These reviews offered over 500 pages of synthesized information documented by almost 2,000 references. Most of these replaced older reviews published in the late 1980s and early 1990s. For example, a review on mule deer published in 1991 included information from 58 references; the 2013 review on mule deer synthesized up-to-date information from 372 references. Other species reviews published this year covered northern goshawk, Florida scrub jay, white-tailed deer, thimbleberry, and redosier dogwood.

In addition to species reviews, four Fire Studies were published in FEIS in 2013, including a

Top figure: Florida scrub jay. Photo by Christina Macon, Florida Department of Environmental Protection. Bottom figure: Redosier dogwood. Photo courtesy of Steven Katovich, U.S. Forest Service, Bugwood.org.

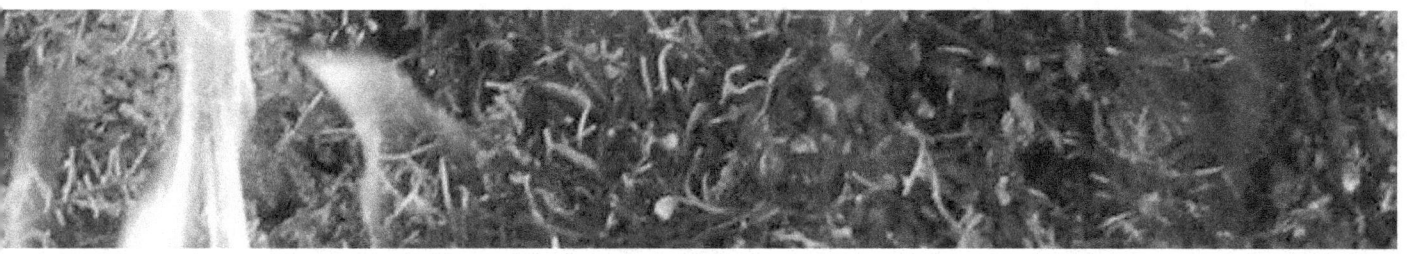

Laboratory and documented in the Citation Retrieval System (CRS). CRS contains more than 80,000 citations. In 2013, FEIS staff added approximately 1,160 citations to CRS.

Contact: Jane Kapler Smith
FMI Staff: Ilana Abrahamson, Janet Fryer, Corey Gucker, Robin Innes, Nancy McMurray, Rachelle Meyer, Jane Kapler Smith, Katharine Stone, Kris Zouhar
Collaborators: Charlotte M. Reemts (The Nature Conservancy), Christie Sclafani (Pacific Southwest Research Station), Department of Interior, National Wildfire Coordinating Group's Fuels Management Committee
Status: Ongoing
Publications: 14 Species Reviews and 4 Fire Studies published at http://www.feis-crs.org/beta/

Management Project Summary that was written in conjunction with The Nature Conservancy in Texas. The Fire Studies completed in FEIS this year included fire effects information on 93 species reviewed in FEIS and added information on 79 additional species.

Literature used for FEIS reviews is stored in the Fire Effects Library at the Missoula Fire Sciences

Top figure: Mule deer buck. Photo courtesy of Robert Sivinski, CalPhotos. Bottom left figure Northern goshawk. Photo by Nathan Stone. Bottom right figure White-tailed deer. Photo courtesy of Charlie Barker, Wind Cave National Park.

Fire Regime Syntheses in the Fire Effects Information System

Managers and planners need scientifically sound, up-to-date information on historical fire regimes. To address managers' needs for syntheses of the growing body of research on historical fire regimes, the FMI Information Team developed and showcased a new product, the Fire Regime Synthesis, in the Fire Effects Information System (FEIS, http://www.feis-crs.org/beta/) during 2013.

Fire Regime Syntheses bring together information from two sources: the scientific literature and Biophysical Settings models and associated geospatial data developed by LANDFIRE (http://www.landfire.gov/). The Biophysical Settings models represent vegetation that may have dominated the landscape prior to Euro-American settlement.

Fire Regime Syntheses provide consistent, current information to the management community on historical (presettlement) fire regimes and contemporary changes in fuels and fire regimes; supplement information on individual species' adaptations and responses to fire provided by FEIS species reviews; and enable LANDFIRE to incorporate the latest science on historical fire regimes into data revisions and identify regions and plant community types lacking fire history data.

Fire Regime Syntheses present current information on historical fire frequency, spatial pattern, extent, and seasonality; historical natural and human-caused ignition sources; and typical patterns of fire intensity and severity. The syntheses also provide information on contemporary changes in fuels, especially in relation to their potential to influence fire regimes. This discussion addresses possible influences from invasive species and climate change. Each Fire Regime Synthesis links to related species reviews in FEIS. In the future, the species reviews will be linked back to Fire Regime Syntheses so up-date-date fire regime information will be available for all 1,100 Species Reviews in FEIS.

Fire Regime Syntheses are now available for all of Hawai'i and for Alaskan tundra and Alaskan coastal communities. More syntheses will be added to FEIS in the coming year.

Contacts: Jane Kapler Smith, Robin Innes
Collaborators: Kori Blankenship (The Nature Conservancy), Don Long (LANDFIRE), Jim Menakis (WO FAM), Interagency Fuels Management Committee
Status: Ongoing
Publications: 3 Fire Regime Syntheses published at http://www.feis-crs.org/beta/

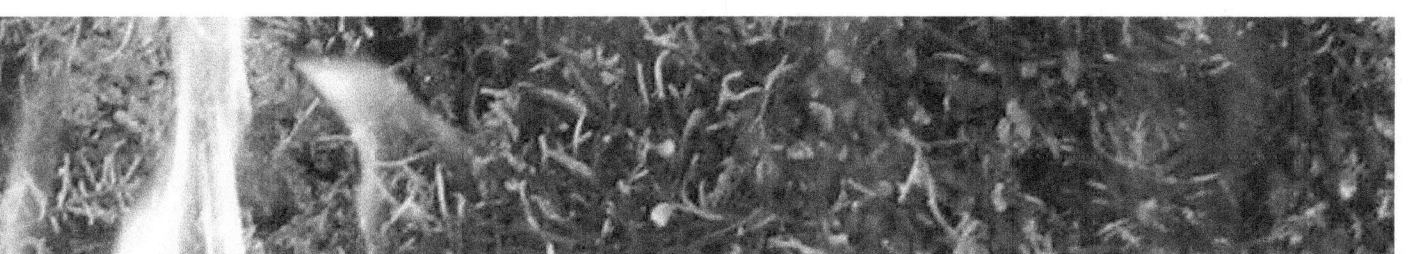

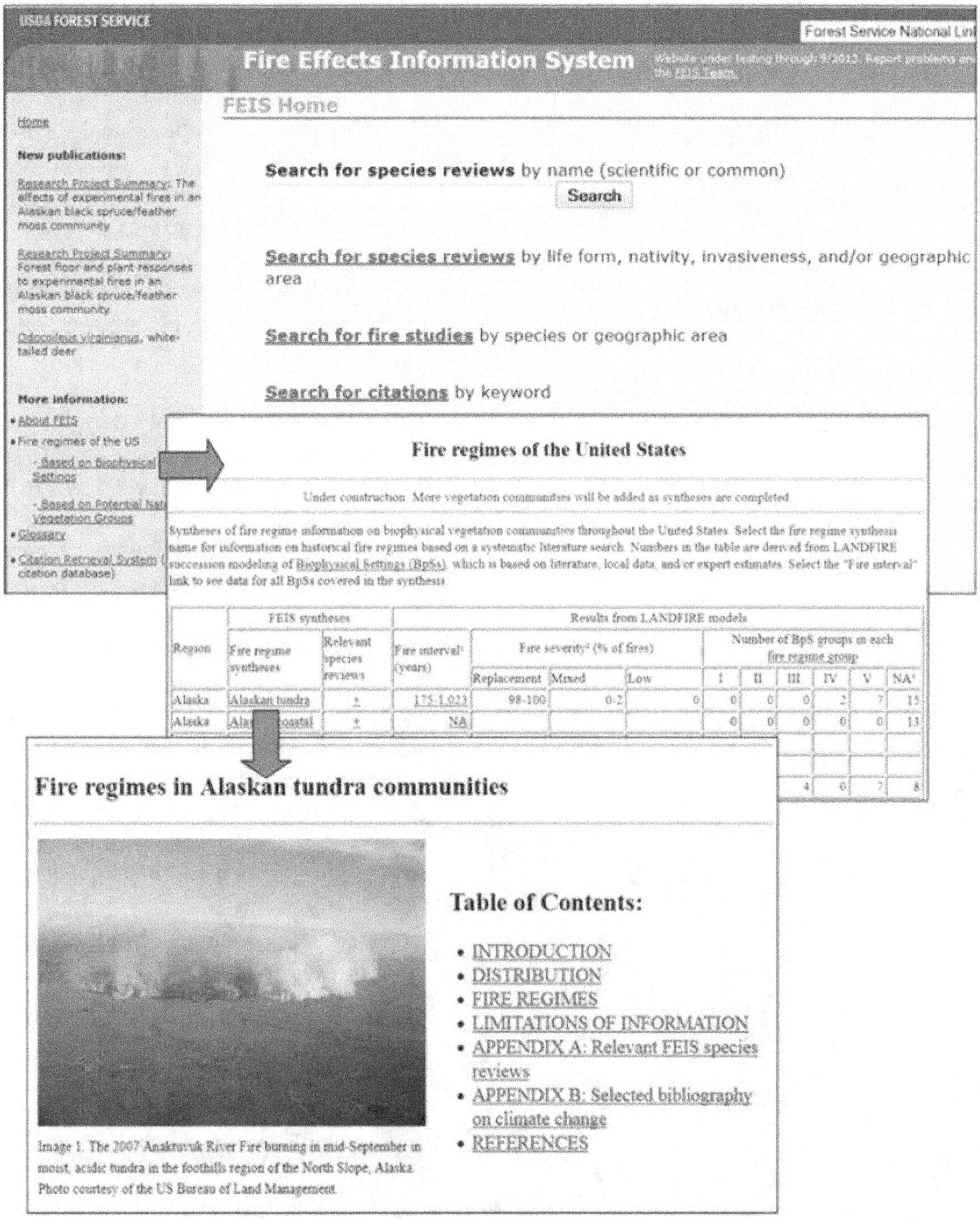

Figure: To access Fire Regime Syntheses in FEIS, click on "Fire regimes of the U.S. based on Biophysical Settings" in the left-hand margin.

Information Team

Outreach to Students and Educators

The Missoula Fire Sciences Laboratory's Conservation Education Program provides tours, curriculum, teacher workshops, and presentations to increase the public's understanding of wildland fire science. FMI contributes to this effort in many ways.

Future Fire Science Managers

For students in grades 3-12, FMI staff provided tours of the Missoula Fire Sciences Laboratory (Fire Lab) for approximately 250 students and 15 teachers and other adults in 2013. Tours included activities on fire safety, fire spread, fire ecology, and potential careers in fire research. One tour for high school students from Browning, MT, investigated the flaming and smoldering properties of different kinds of wood used in traditional fire carriers. While attending the Fifth International Fire Congress in Portland, OR, FMI staff visited two elementary schools near Salem, OR, introducing students in Kindergarten and Grades 4-5 to the FireWorks curriculum, a curriculum and trunk filled with materials for hands-on activities that explore the physical and biological sciences of wildland fire. This curriculum includes topics in fire safety, fire physics, and fire ecology. FMI staff also collaborated with teachers to test an Internet-based learning activity that explores the probability of fire and fire effects based on various climate, development, fuel treatment, and fire management scenarios.

For college students, FMI staff demonstrated principles of fire behavior at the Traditional Knowledge Workshop sponsored by the Northern Rockies Fire Science Consortium at Salish Kootenai College, Pablo, MT. FMI staff also presented information on the Fire Effects Information System to a fire science class at the University of Montana. Undergraduate students from the University of Idaho visit the Fire Lab annually as part of their fire behavior and fire and fuel modeling courses, while students from the University of Montana toured the Fire Lab and spoke with FMI researchers about current research. Students from the University of Kentucky pursuing graduate research in fire sciences visited FMI staff and used equipment available only at the Fire Lab.

Professional Development

FMI provided a two-day teacher workshop for teachers and agency educators on the FireWorks curriculum. They also provided a one-

Figure: Teachers at the FireWorks master class use feltboard materials to tell the story of lodgpole pine's relationship with fire.

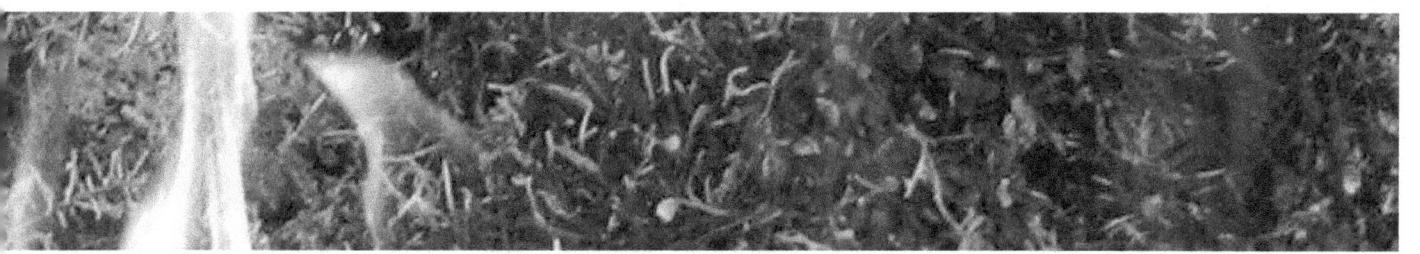

Fire Danger Rating System and Geospatial Fire Analysis Interpretation and Application (S-495). Regional courses, taught in the Northern Rockies and Great Basin, included Introduction to Fire Effects (RX-310), Smoke Management Techniques (RX-410), Advanced Fire Behavior Calculations (S-490), and Intermediate National Fire Danger Rating System (S-491).

Public Outreach

FMI researchers and staff provided tours and science demonstrations to members of the general public, agency administrators, and international visitors. These tours showcased the breadth of work done at the Fire Lab, including research performed in the combustion chamber and wind tunnel.

Contact: Kristine Lee
Collaborator: RMRS Fire, Fuel, and Smoke Science Program
Status: Ongoing

hour demonstration of the FireWorks curriculum for fire science professionals at the Fifth International Fire Congress and demonstrated principles of fire behavior at teacher workshops sponsored by the Glacier Institute and "A Forest for Every Classroom" program.

Agency personnel from the U.S. Forest Service, Bureau of Land Management, and National Park Service participated in a mentorship program with FMI, in which they learned details of operational fire modeling systems such as FlamMap that are specifically tailored to their home units. University researchers and a research scientist from Bulgaria also participated in the mentorship program, increasing their knowledge of fire behavior modeling in their local areas.

Members of FMI also instructed a number of regional and national courses administered by the National Wildland Fire Coordinating Group. National-level courses included Advanced National

Figure: Teachers and agency fire specialists investigate fuel properties at the FireWorks master class.

Modeling Team

BehavePlus Fire Modeling System Support

The BehavePlus fire modeling system is a nationally supported desktop application that produces tables, graphs, and simple diagrams of modeled fire behavior, fire effects, and fire environment. BehavePlus is used to model surface and crown fire spread rate and intensity, transition from surface to crown fire, fire size, effect of containment efforts, tree scorch height and mortality, fuel moisture, wind adjustment factor, spotting distance, and more.

BehavePlus is not limited to a specific application, but rather is designed to be used for any fire management application for which fire model results are useful. It is used by federal, state, and local land management agencies, universities, consultants, and others. Outputs from BehavePlus are used for a range of applications including wildfire prediction, prescribed fire planning, and fuel hazard assessment, as well as communication, education, and training.

FMI staff led classroom and online training sessions on BehavePlus in 2013. A total of 35 participants from a variety of government agencies and universities participated in these sessions. In addition, a workshop was held in northern Montana to prepare approximately 13 students for the Advanced Fire Behavior Calculations (S-490) course, in which BehavePlus is extensively used.

BehavePlus is currently being updated to include more than 20 new and improved features, including new analysis variables and special case fuel models.

An agreement between Washington Office Fire and Aviation Management (WO FAM) and FMI ensures FMI staff is available to assist the National Fire Applications Help Desk in answering questions regarding BehavePlus operation. In 2013, FMI staff responded to more than 20 technical support contacts.

Contact: Faith Ann Heinsch
FMI Staff: Pat Andrews (retired), Faith Ann Heinsch, LaWen Hollingsworth
Contract Programmer: Systems for Environmental Management
Status: Ongoing

Figure: BehavePlus fire modeling system logo.

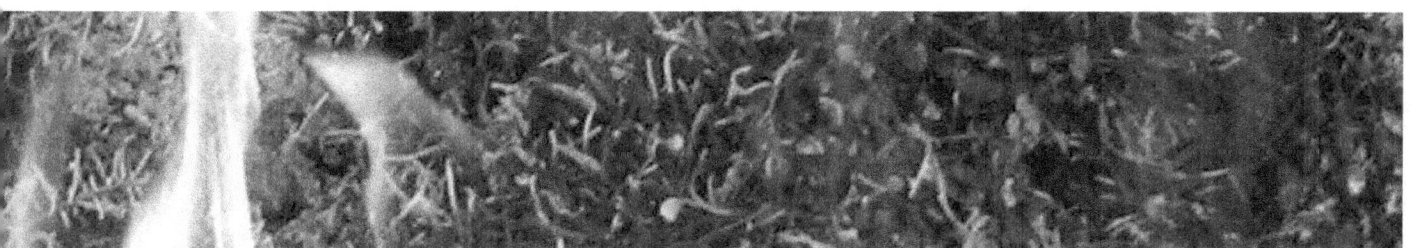

Fire Danger Characteristics Charts

A fire characteristics chart is a graph that represents either U.S. National Fire Danger Rating System (NFDRS) indices or fire behavior characteristics (surface fire or crown fire). The NFDRS and the operational fire behavior systems (such as BehavePlus and FARSITE: Fire Area Simulator) are based on the same fundamental mathematical fire models. This relationship makes fire characteristics charts possible. The Fire Characteristics Chart software program was developed to produce fire characteristics charts for both fire danger and fire behavior. Charts produced by the program can be included in briefings, reports, and presentations.

The fire behavior characteristics chart was released in 2012. This chart shows the relationship among rate of spread, flame length, fireline intensity, and heat per unit area. It helps communicate and interpret modeled or observed fire behavior. Example fire behavior applications include fire model understanding, observed crown fire behavior, ignition pattern effect on fire behavior, prescribed fire planning, briefings, and case studies. Separate charts are available for surface fire and crown fire because of differences in the flame length model used for each.

The fire danger characteristics chart was released in 2013. This chart displays the relationship among three NFDRS indices (Spread Component, Energy Release Component, and Burning Index) by plotting

their values as a single point. Indices calculated by FireFamilyPlus, an application used for analysis of fire danger indices and weather, can be imported into the Fire Characteristics Chart program. Example applications include comparing fire seasons, weather stations, and fuel models.

Contact: Faith Ann Heinsch
FMI Staff: Pat Andrews (retired)
Contract Programmer: Systems for Environmental Management
Status: Ongoing

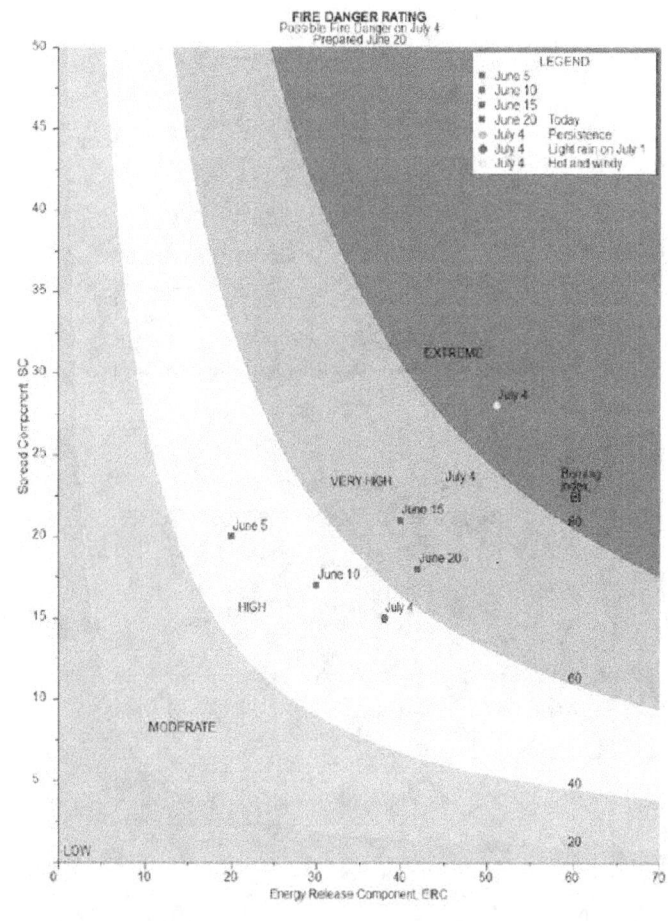

Figure: A sample fire danger characteristics chart showing past fire danger rating and three possible forecasts for fire danger.

FireFamilyPlus 4.1

FireFamilyPlus 4.1 was officially accepted and released in June 2013. FireFamilyPlus is an agency-independent desktop application that supports the spectrum of analysis tools required by fire managers to successfully use the U.S. National Fire Danger Rating System (NFDRS). It can be used to calculate historical fire danger rating indices and components and summarize both fire and weather data. The program can statistically analyze historical relationships between fire danger indices and fire occurrence, displaying data in various formats. It also generates the Fire Danger Rating Pocketcards required by the 30-Mile Abatement Plan and supports Predictive Services' functions at all Geographic Coordination Centers.

FireFamilyPlus is the computational and analysis cornerstone of the the biennial Advanced Fire Danger Rating course at the National Advanced Fire and Resource Institute (NAFRI) and annual Intermediate Fire Danger Rating (S-491) courses held by the various Geographic Area Training

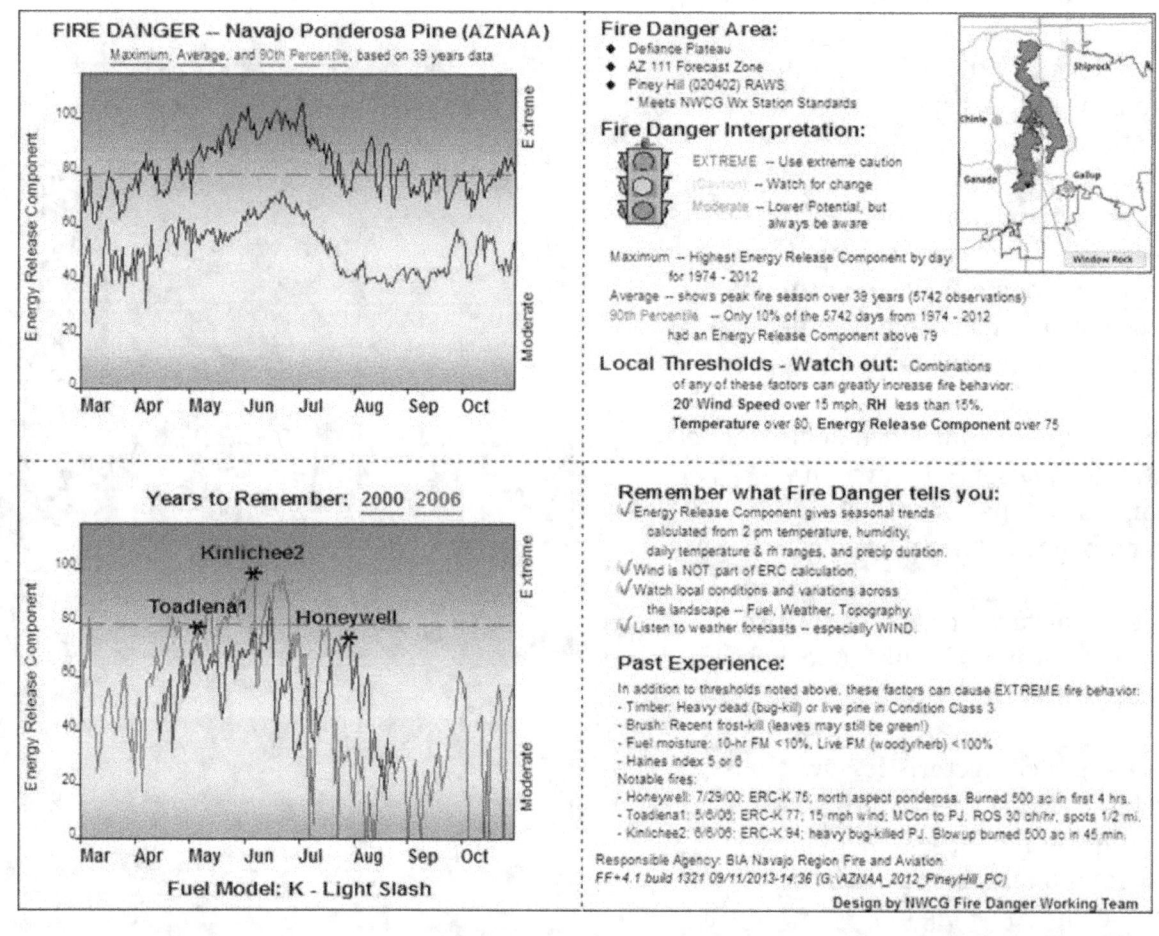

Figure: A Pocketcard, given to firefighters to aid in understanding local fire danger, can be produced with FireFamilyPlus. Image courtesy of the Bureau of Indian Affairs.

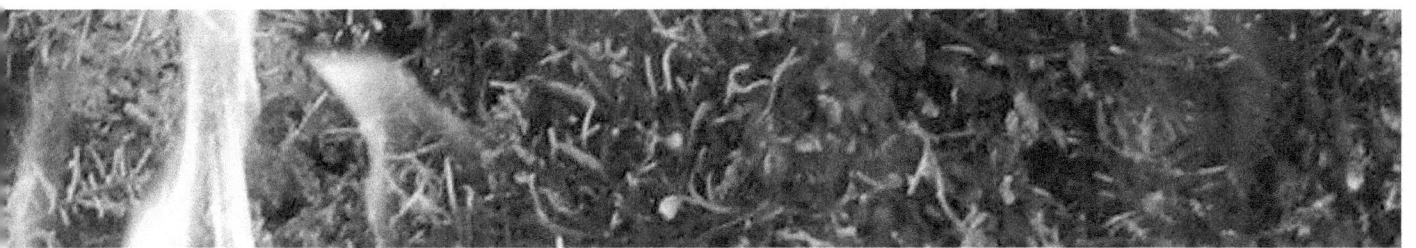

Centers throughout the country. It also provides climate summaries for techniques taught in the Long Term Fire Risk Assessment course (S-495) at NAFRI.

The updated version includes new analysis variables, new station metadata, new processing options, a weather term module, and numerous fixes and enhancements. One of the most significant functional elements of the update is aligning of NFDRS processing with recent changes in the Weather Information Management System (WIMS) that virtually eliminates missing observations and supports a new data transfer format (FW13) that includes solar radiation, wind gust, and snow flag fields. A Service Level Agreement between Washington Office Fire and Aviation Management (WO FAM) and FMI ensures FMI scientists are available to assist the National Fire Applications Help Desk in answering questions regarding FireFamilyPlus operation. In 2013, FMI staff responded to more than 25 elevated tickets on FireFamilyPlus technical issues.

FMI Lead: Larry Bradshaw
Contract Programmer: Systems for Environmental Management
Agency Contact: Larry Bradshaw (FMI)
Status: Ongoing

Fire Incident Support

FMI staff provides fuels and fire behavior modeling, operations, and planning support during fire incidents occurring throughout the nation. In 2013, FMI staff contributed more than 880 hours in support of fire incidents in the U.S. Forest Service Northern Region (Region 1), Rocky Mountain Region (Region 2), Southwestern Region (Region 3), and Intermountain Region (Region 4). In addition, FMI Fire Spatial Analyst Chuck McHugh provided analysis in support of the Serious Accident Investigation report of the Yarnell Hill fatalities. Nineteen firefighters died on the Yarnell Hill Fire in central Arizona on June 30, 2013, after deploying fire shelters.

FMI Leads: Faith Ann Heinsch, LaWen Hollingsworth, W. Matt Jolly, Chuck McHugh
Collaborator: RMRS Fire, Fuel, and Smoke Science Program
Agency Contact: Kristine Lee (FMI)
Status: Ongoing

Figure: Fire moves toward Hells Half Acre Lookout from Lunch Creek and Hells Half Acre Creek on the Gold Pan Complex Fire, one of the fires that FMI staff provided support for in 2013. Photo courtesy of Risa Lange-Navarro, Bitterroot National Forest.

Modeling Team

Fire Management in Nepal

In April 2013, Forester and Spatial Fire Analyst Chuck McHugh spent two weeks in Nepal providing comment and review of the Nepalese fire management program. His visit was coordinated with U.S. Forest Service International Programs, the U.S Agency for International Development (USAID), the U.S. Department of State, and World Wildlife Fund Nepal (WWF Nepal). He presented materials during a workshop and gave three other presentations to a variety of audiences including members of USAID, WWF Nepal, Embassy of the United States Kathmandu, Nepal's Ministry of Forests and Soil Conservation (MoFSC), Nepal Police, local Community Forest User Groups (CFUGs), and the Nepal Institute of Forestry. He also visited several Forest Districts where he met with local managers, reviewed projects focused on reducing fire risk, and observed CFUGs suppressing active fires.

The workshop was attended by 30 senior officials from Bangladesh, Bhutan, India, Myanmar, Nepal, and Pakistan. McHugh was joined by experts from the U.S. Forest Service Remote Sensing

The primary objectives of the visit were to 1) attend the "Developing Forest Adaptation Strategies under Changing Climate Scenarios: Geospatial Support Systems for Improved Forest Fire Management" workshop and present an invited talk on "Geospatial Decision Support Tools for Modeling Wildland Fire"; 2) provide targeted technical support and comments regarding fire and fire management on the USAID-WWF Nepal funded Hariyo Ban Project; and 3) provide comments and observations to MoFSC regarding fire management issues in Nepal.

Top figure: On April 15, 2013, Chuck McHugh visited a recent wildfire on the Kapilvastu Forest District with the district fire crew, unit foresters, and WWF Nepal. Note burned area in the background, left. Bottom figure: Local Community Forest User Group (CFUG) observed on a wildfire along the East-West Highway on the Rupandehi Forest District on April 16, 2013. This CFUG had not received any basic firefighting training or equipment.

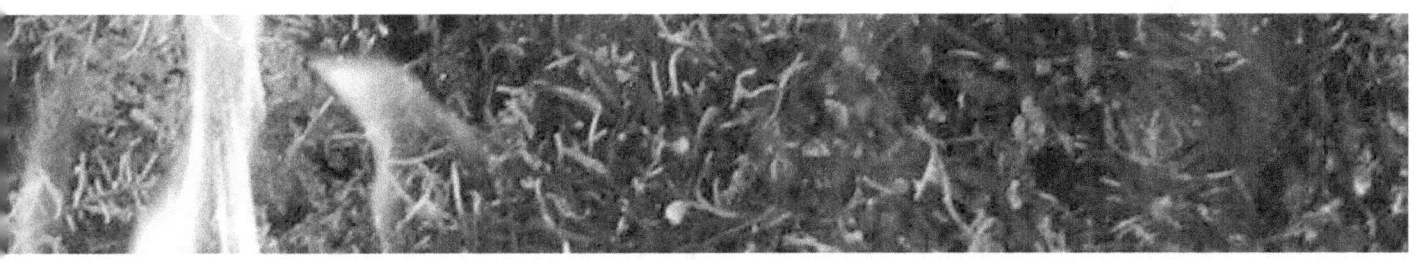

of technical training on operational forest fire detection and monitoring systems followed by a day-long discussion on fire and forest management policy. The workshop helped identify gaps in technology, capacity, and policy in the Hindu Kush Himalayan region and foster regional cooperation for improving forest fire management.

Chuck McHugh concluded his trip with a formal briefing to MoFSC on his observations of fire and fire management in the country. He concluded that although Nepal faces many challenges as it continues to develop its fire management policy and response, these challenges offer

Applications Center (RSAC), NASA, and SERVIR-Himalaya, an initiative at the International Centre for Integrated Mountain Development (ICIMOD) supported by USAID. The event included two days

many opportunities to address issues and formulate policy and strategies specific to Nepal's unique circumstances.

Contact: Chuck McHugh
Collaborators: U.S. Forest Service International Programs, USAID, U.S. Department of State, and WWF Nepal
Status: Completed

Top figure: Visit with the Raniban Community Forest User Group (CFUG) on the Kaski Forest District on April 17, 2013. This CFUG received basic firefighting training and equipment provided by WWF Nepal. Bottom figure: Chuck McHugh provided a formal briefing to the Secretary, Under Secretary, and other officials within the Ministry of Forests and Soil Conservation, Kathmandu, Nepal, on April 18, 2013.

Modeling Team

Modeling Fire Danger for Sandia National Laboratories

Sandia National Laboratories, located at the Kirtland Air Force Base in Albuquerque, NM, conducts tests at its Aerial Cable Facility and Burn Site (ACF) in conjunction with a land use agreement between Kirtland Air Force Base and the U.S. Forest Service. Historically, Kirtland Air Force Base set the National Fire Danger Rating level for the area one level above that of the nearby U.S. Forest Service, Sandia Ranger District, which uses observations from a Remote Automated Weather Station (RAWS) for computing daily fire danger rating across the District.

Kirtland Air Force Base worked with FMI Physical Scientist Faith Ann Heinsch and FMI Meteorologist Larry Bradshaw to develop more accurate fire danger ratings for the Sandia National Laboratories. These researchers compared site-specific data and fire danger ratings for the Sandia Ranger District's RAWS, the National Weather Service's weather station in Albuquerque, the Old School House weather station, and a Fire Program Analysis grid point to develop climatology and fire business thresholds specific to the ACF. FireFamilyPlus was used to calculate fire danger rating indices and components for comparison with fire occurrence data. Fire occurrence data from 1995-2011 were combined with weather data to determine potential thresholds for fire danger at the study site.

Results from this study provided insights into the fire danger of the area. Fire danger ratings developed using the Old School House weather station, the closest weather station to ACF, and RAWS were different but showed similar trends; they were most divergent during March through June, the active fire season. Preliminary results from this study indicated that the previous plan was overly restrictive. Results from this study will be used by Sandia National Laboratories to develop a fire danger operating plan for their facility that more accurately represents the fire danger of the area. This new plan should increase the number of test days while maintaining operational restrictions when necessary for safety.

Contact: Larry Bradshaw
FMI Staff: Larry Bradshaw, Faith Ann Heinsch
Collaborator: Sandia National Laboratories
Status: Completed
Publication: Bradshaw, L.; Heinsch, F. A. 2012. Final report for the fire danger modeling work agreement between USFS, Rocky Mountain Research Station and Sandia National Laboratories. Missoula, MT: U.S. Department of Agriculture, Forest Service, Rocky Mountain Research Station. 36 p.

Figure: Location of the Aerial Cable Facility and Burn Site (ACF) and four weather datasets included in analyses (National Weather Service's Albuquerque Forecast Office (KABQ), Old School House, U.S. Forest Service's Remote Automated Weather Station (291402 - Oak Flats), and a Fire Program Analysis grid point (FPA Grid Point 19, 176)).

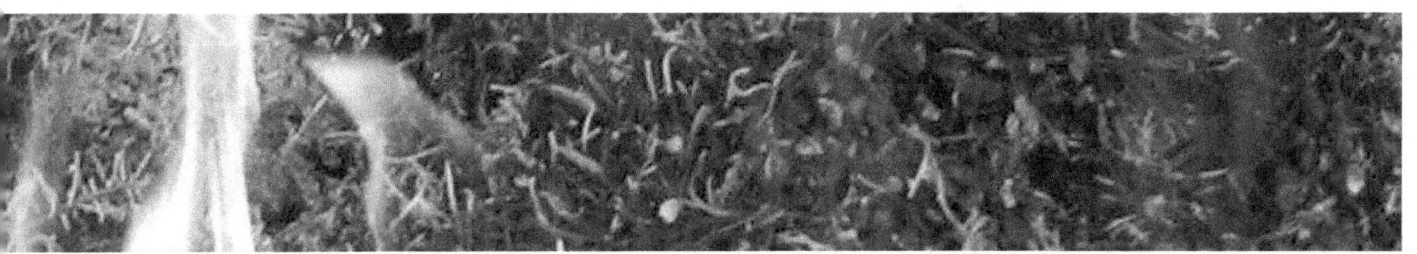

Weather Information Management System Development and Support

The U.S. National Fire Danger Rating System (NFDRS) is used by all federal and most state fire management agencies for assessing seasonal fire severity across the nation. The application that hosts the NFDRS is the Washington Office Fire and Aviation Management's (WO FAM) Weather Information Management System (WIMS) located at the USDA National Information Technology Center in Kansas City, Missouri. WIMS ingests hourly weather observations from more than 1,800 Remote Automated Weather Stations (RAWS) across the continental United States, Alaska, Hawaii, and Puerto Rico.

In 2013, FMI staff collaborated with WO FAM program managers to establish design documents for replacing the existing Live Fuel Moisture model used in the NFDRS with the Growing Season Index developed by FMI Research Ecologist W. Matt Jolly.

FMI staff also worked with the Fire Danger Subcommittee of the National Wildfire Coordinating Group's Fire Environment Committee to approve and implement a new fire weather data exchange format (FW13). This format virtually eliminates problematic missing days from the historical WIMS daily archive and adds solar radiation and wind gust information long requested by users of the historical data. The FW13 format has been implemented in WIMS, FireFamilyPlus, and the long-term repository of hourly RAWS data at the Western Region Climate Center.

FMI staff provides national technical support for WIMS through the National Fire Applications Help Desk. In 2013, they responded to 35 elevated tickets on WIMS technical issues.

Contact: Larry Bradshaw
FMI Staff: Larry Bradshaw, Faith Ann Heinsch, W. Matt Jolly
Collaborators: National Interagency Fuels, Fire, and Vegetation Technology Transfer (NIFTT), Predictive Services, National Wildfire Coordinating Group's Fire Danger Subcommittee, National Weather Service
Status: Ongoing

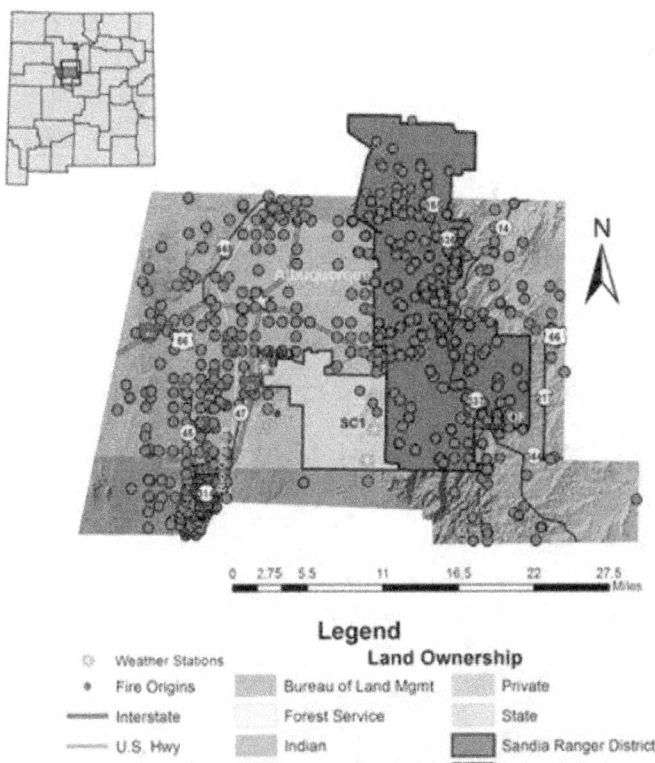

Legend

Land Ownership

○ Weather Stations	
● Fire Origins	Bureau of Land Mgmt	Private
—— Interstate	Forest Service	State
—— U.S. Hwy	Indian	Sandia Ranger District
—— N.M. Hwy	National Park Service	Dept. of Defense

Figure: Fires occurrence data from 1995-2011 and local weather data were combined to determine potential thresholds for fire danger at the Sandia National Laboratories.

Modeling Team

National Fire Danger Rating System Development and Support

The U.S. National Fire Danger Rating System (NFDRS) is a system used by wildland fire management agencies to assess current fire danger at local, regional and national levels. It consists of a variety of indices that portray current potential fire danger conditions. FMI staff has been highly involved in the development and application of NFDRS for decades. In 2013, they continued to develop and enhance the base fire danger model and the distribution platforms that make fire danger information available to fire managers.

The Wildland Fire Assessment System (WFAS) is an integrated, web-based resource to support fire management decisions. It serves as the primary distribution platform for spatial fire danger data to a nationwide user base of federal, state, and local land managers. This web-based platform saw over 39,000 unique visitors during 2013. The system provides multi-temporal and multi-spatial views of fire weather and fire potential, including fuel moistures and fire danger classes from the NFDRS, as well as Keetch-Byram and Palmer drought indices, lower atmospheric stability

indicators, and satellite-derived vegetation conditions. It also provides fire potential forecasts from 24 hours to 30 days.

In 2013, WFAS developers in FMI worked closely with researchers from the University of Idaho, the University of Montana, and U.S. Forest Service Region 1 to develop the TOPOFIRE web display and analysis system (http://topofire.dbs.umt.edu). This system is used for processing and displaying spatial weather data that can be used to support the development of the next generation of NFDRS and WFAS. The project is supported by NASA Earth Sciences Applications and is aimed at streamlining the development and use of spatial data for wildland fire decision making. The system will provide access to a wealth of high-resolution spatial weather data that will significantly enhance WFAS products.

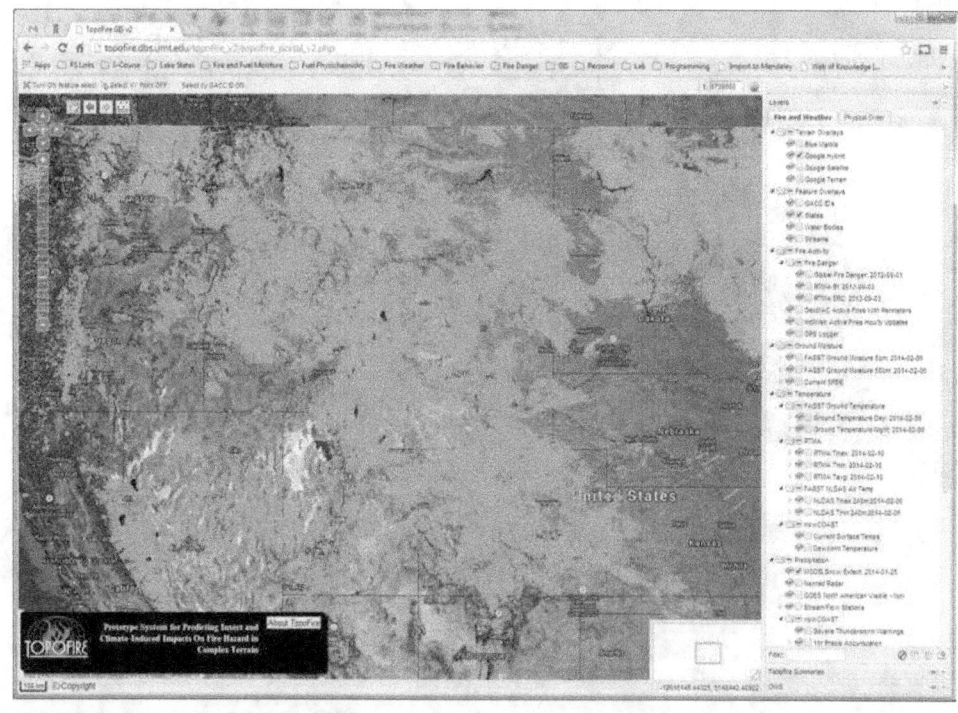

Figure: MODIS snow cover map for western Montana from the TOPOFIRE web display and analysis system. The TOPOFIRE web display and analysis system now provides WFAS with access to MODIS satellite-derived snow cover extent in real-time. These maps can be integrated into the U.S. National Fire Danger Rating System to regulate heavy dead fuel moisture calculations.

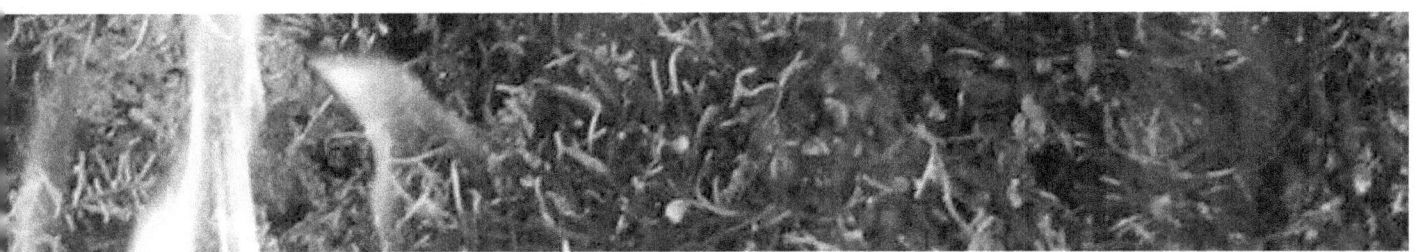

WFAS developers in FMI have been producing fire danger forecasts from the National Weather Service's National Digital Forecast Database (NDFD) for several years. WFAS developers continued to work closely with Predictive Services' meteorologists throughout the country in 2013 to provide point forecasts for key Remote Automated Weather Stations (RAWS) located throughout the United States. WFAS now produces seven-day outlooks daily for over 1,000 weather station points. These outlooks are being used operationally to produce seven-day fire potential forecasts for every geographic area in the continental United States. These seven-day forecasts provide a much longer fire danger outlook than was previously available and are providing fire managers with tools to meet strategic planning needs. The point forecast interface that produces the seven-day fire danger forecasts from the NDFD can be accessed at http://www.wfas.net/.

WFAS developers in FMI have also designed and implemented a state-of-the-art web mapping interface for the display and analysis of remotely sensed spatial fire potential data. This new interface allows the rapid assessment of fuel conditions across a landscape, and it provides managers with several tools to assess fuel changes over time. The system is built on a suite of open-source tools that provides a means for efficient storage, display, and analysis of large spatial datasets. This new framework will be a building block for a new, integrated fire danger display and analysis system. The new interface complements the existing static LANDFIRE national maps and will provide more system flexibility by allowing users to define their own area of interest, link to weather station data in a tabular format, and perform searches for map features. The prototype for the interactive map can be accessed at http://maps.wfas.net/. This web mapping and analysis interface will provide the tools necessary for the rapid and effective dissemination of large spatial datasets to the fire management community and will ultimately serve as the development platform for the next generation of fire danger rating systems.

In addition to development and maintenance of the NFDRS, FMI staff participated as core instructors for Intermediate NFDRS (S-491), National Advanced NFDRS, and associated Weather Information Management System (WIMS) courses during 2013. Approximately 250 participants from a variety of state and federal government agencies and universities participated in these training sessions.

Lastly, FMI staff provides national technical support for the NFDRS and associated programs through the National Fire Applications Help Desk and responded to over 45 elevated tickets on technical issues in 2012.

Contacts: Larry Bradshaw, W. Matt Jolly
FMI Staff: Larry Bradshaw, Faith Ann Heinsch, W. Matt Jolly
Collaborators: National Interagency Fuels, Fire, and Vegetation Technology Transfer (NIFTT), National Wildfire Coordinating Group's Fire Danger Subcommittee, National Weather Service, Predictive Services
Status: Seven-day fire potential forecasts complete; collaboration with TOPOFIRE project ongoing; support and technology transfer ongoing.